Praise

How to

"Walking on air is a
bit about research, scary stuff." – Richard Allinson,
Presenter, BBC Radio 2.

"Clever guide for those wishing to start, or break into
bigger things. I wish this book was around when I
started in radio." – Simon Hirst, Presenter, Capital
FM, Yorkshire

"This book is a wake-up call about adapting to
territory and contains valuable mind-sets on the
current science of broadcasting." – Bruno Brookes,
former Radio 1 DJ and CEO, Immedia Broadcast
PLC

"It would take someone years to learn the
fundamentals contained within." – Leona Graham,
Presenter, Absolute Radio.

"I wish this book was around 20 years ago when I
worked on Hospital Radio dreaming of working at
Capital..." – Tony Dibbin, Programme Director, Gold
Radio Network

"I wish I wrote that." – Kam Kelly, Capital
Breakfast, Wales.

"Packed with shocking truths that will save people
years." – Sam Pinkham, presenter, Gem 106

Walking On-Air

How to be a Radio Presenter

Radio Talent

Published by Radio Talent at Smashwords

Copyright 2013

FOREWORD

I was 18 years of age in the long hot summer of '77 and I'd just acquired my first FAL Disco twin deck with twin speakers and lights. The whole package was £200, a fortune in those days but I thought of it as an investment in my future although I had no idea where that first purchase would take me. I just loved disco music and any thought of being a radio presenter was some way off.

It was three years later before that broadcasting dream came to fruition with a stint at BBC Radio Carlisle, as it was once known. I soon realised that all the hours I had spent behind those sweaty disco desks counted for nothing. In a radio studio, everything was so very different. There was no audience to see; just an empty room, a mic and a few records and I struggled to come up with things to say. This was bad because radio is simply a communications business and to stand a chance in this world, I had to learn how to do this and fast. More than anything, I needed to know how this all worked.

Like all great art a new skill takes time to master but some are also lucky enough to have a great teacher. If you can find one that is kind enough to spend time teaching you then ropes, structures, preparation and planning so much the better. Not everyone had this.

I was lucky in that I had good 'ears'. The very best radio talent not only know what to do they also know the mechanics of it all. They have spent time listening to themselves but also to others right across the spectrum of radio. I was always fascinated by phraseology and structure, but more than anything I wanted to learn the art of preparation. I soon noticed that those presenters that prepared well, very often performed at a far higher level than their competitors and that is still the same today.

Although individuality is the golden key to success you can do nothing if you don't know the rules first. Consider it your driving test for radio. If you read this book carefully and take on board it's many valid and careful suggestions from vastly experienced hands, you can pass your basic radio test with ease.

Digest its contents and you will be ready to take radio forward in your own style and in your own way. It is a radio bible of sorts. It is the kind of shortcut I wish I had when I first set off on this journey. Believe me, there is no shortcut to success in a medium where the art of communication is vital. You have to learn the basic skills first and this wonderful book will help you get there and a lot faster than I did. If you mix this information with a love of the medium alongside your own individuality, you won't go far wrong.

John Myers

John is the Chair of the prestigious Sony Radio Academy Awards and is the former CEO of the Radio Academy, a registered charity dedicated to the encouragement, recognition and promotion of excellence in UK radio broadcasting and audio production. He was once described by BBC Radio 2 presenter Jeremy Vine as being "probably the most important figure in commercial radio since Marconi" He has also authored the book Team - It's only Radio which is available via www.myersmedia.co.uk

Table of Contents

Introduction

Becoming a radio presenter is easier than you think. Like learning any new skill, all you need is the right Intel, and this is what you are about to learn. If you can be flexible in your approach and can absorb the information in this short book, you will be well on your way to being better informed than most people in your position.

All the inside secrets of radio you are about to learn, come from high profile presenters and radio management. The material has been assembled from personal career blunders, business meetings and countless radio training sessions. It has also been compiled from numerous interviews with radio decision makers, award winning talent, and celebrities.

Your perceptions about radio are going to change, and we are about to share cutting edge information that will make very a powerful impact on your future. Books should be treated as though they are valuable treasures; this is because they allow you to access people's vast experience in just a few pages. In our book, we hope to offer valuable wisdom for not just complete beginners, but semi professionals and even seasoned experts.

Without too much preamble, let's get down to business. The first, and possibly most important thing you will learn in this book, is this--radio is a business. It is entertainment, yes, but all radio, whether commercial or public service, carries an agenda alongside entertainment. The agenda might be generating revenue, attracting listeners or providing a service in accordance with a licence. Without spoiling the mystique of radio, appreciating that there is more to it than just entertainment will provide you with a mind-set that will beneficial as you develop your career in the industry.

Take the movie business for example. Many will tell you that it exists only to make money. Much to the frustration of passionate movie buffs, fewer and fewer movies, especially in Hollywood, are made today in the name of "art" and many more are made simply to generate money; sequels to financially successful films are an illustration of this unfortunate reality. The world's greatest script is completely useless if a studio can't make money from it.

Harsh and as cynical as this perspective might seem at first, learning to study or identify how or why things make money has its advantages, particularly if you want to make money yourself.

Watching TV is another example. To some people, they watch TV and enjoy the programmes. Others know that what they are really doing is watching people earn money doing what they love. The actors in a TV show are all following a career path, as are the cameramen, the editors, the producers, the writers and all the thousands of people that make up the parts of a show. They are all earning money making a show that has to make money to be there. Bottom line: as entertaining as TV and movies are, it's a business.

When you apply this thought process to everything, it can be quite mind-blowing. You might be reading this in a Starbucks, which is a business. Even the chair you are sitting on is a business, as is the person winning the janitorial contract to clean it after hours, and so it goes on.

When we listen to the radio there are more things happening behind the scenes than we might initially think. A station has to make money or it can't survive. A presenter is just a cog in a giant wheel. And our job here, through this book, is to get you to be one of the best cogs ever.

In this book, we will challenge you to genuinely understand the people or companies you want to work with. In life, the more you understand people, the easier life becomes. Similarly, in business, the more you understand your customer, the more you sell. In radio, the more you understand a station and its intentions, the more successful you will be.

Success is often formulaic. A large proportion of career success is derived from learning how the wheels turn in your chosen business and making the right moves. However, when we set out with a dream, we can often make foolish mistakes by not first understanding what our dream really is. We can spend years wanting to do something without really understanding what it takes or how it works. We hope to avoid you making the mistakes that so many before you have, and this book is here to help you.

Radio is quite an amazing industry and even nowadays as visual technology dominates our lives, it's still remarkable to conceive that information can travel as sound in thin air. Radio almost seems to teleport information, in real time, from the studio to our ears. Sometimes, when we listen to the radio, we easily forget that a person is speaking to us in real time, at that exact moment, directly, from miles and miles away. Astonishing.

It is this unfathomable magic that sometimes makes us treat radio as esoteric, but our purpose here in this book is to simplify it all. Knowing that radio is just a business like any other business helps you perceive it as less mysterious or daunting. Simply viewing it as a business makes it easier for you to identify the right moves and adopt a sensible mind-set.

Types of Radio Presenters

Let's begin our investigation into the business of radio by taking a look at the different categories that can be used to classify radio presenters. In the interests of simplicity and to outline a clear framework for this book, we'll split the types of radio presenters into different categories. Although the industry rarely classifies presenters by type, our classification will help you consider what sort of radio opportunity appeals to you most.

Most professionals are able to draw from any experience they have gained from all areas of presentation but others choose to follow a single path in accordance with their preference or natural talent.

We will explore each type of presentation separately to demonstrate some of the overall skills you will develop as a presenter. In certain places we will suggest ideas for gaining experience in a particular area.

Speech Presenters

Naturally, a speech presenter is one that broadcasts on a station that plays very little or no music. Speech presenters are most often found on talk radio, public service or current affairs stations. The content on air will be either live, recorded or an ingenious combination of both.

In a typical environment, speech presenters have to be prepared for immediate changes to programme material. Although "speech heavy" stations always have content planned well in advance, news and events often prompt sudden changes. Speech presenters therefore ordinarily w an expertise, either naturally or trained, in being able to handle content professionally without preparation.

Speech presenters are knowledgeable in current affairs, politics or any number of specialist subjects. They are eloquent, well-educated and worldly, often benefiting from a background in journalism.

Some speech presenters, such as those on local public service stations, might have a natural talent for callers or phone-ins, and others might have a unique personality or be experts in particular interests. Regardless of their area of specialisation, speech presenters are also able to appeal to a wide demographic; this is particularly clear when listening to talk or phone-in stations. On talk stations, it is utterly captivating to hear a speech presenter devise content so engaging that people are compelled to contribute. It is even more fascinating when these presenters are vigorously contested, opposed or questioned by listeners but remain impartial, balanced and personally detached.

Speech presentation, at high-profile level, requires great expertise. To give you some context on this adept skillset, a speech presenter has to juggle multiple things simultaneously, for instance: talking to time, listening to a caller, driving the desk, staying on topic, taking direction and so on.

Normally, only the most experienced presenters can do this kind of broadcasting well; however, that doesn't need to be the case. The more you know about a subject, the easier it is to talk about it. With the right amount of preparation and study, anyone can be convincing and sound professional.

Getting practice is not impossible either. Student and Internet radio stations often conduct programming with more speech than music, as do community radio stations, smaller fringe stations and local public service stations. There are even specialist Internet stations that cover all manner of niche subjects. A quick search on TuneIn.com or iTunes will show plenty of stations or podcasts that cover your niche subject. Could you be a contributor for them?

Breakfast or late-night shows also tend to be more speech heavy, so if you can get involved with one, you will learn the art of speaking without music, rapidly. Public service stations are useful, too, not only because they carry more speech programming, but also because they use numerous contributors to create a variety of shows that require the skills of journalists, correspondents and reporters, to name a few types of radio professionals involved in public service stations. Numerous contributors could mean more chances for you to learn or apply useful grounding skills.

If you are passionate about discussion, good at starting interesting conversation, or love a good debate, these attributes might be signs of your natural aptitude for becoming a speech presenter. If you have a keen interest in current affairs, politics, sport or a popular hobby, these are also all good signs, as hearing an expert talk on their subject matter can make good radio.

For some people, the idea of talking on the radio without music fills them with fear. They might love the idea of being a speech presenter but worry they don't actually have the worldliness or natural aptitude; this concern is completely normal and not necessarily a sign that this type of work is not for you. For others, the idea is exhilarating and inspiring, and the idea of discussing a wide variety of different subjects every day fills them with optimism. For everyone, however, speech presentation is simply just a little more than really knowing your subject.

There is most certainly a great sense of satisfaction that comes from working in speech radio: the contentment of knowing you are mastering an intricate art, the feeling of contribution when creating unique and varied content and the pleasure of feeding your brain with new and different information every day.

Like developing any new skill, the first step is to absorb as much of it as you can. Immerse yourself in speech radio and research stations that broadcast the content you are interested in. The more you immerse yourself in speech radio, the easier you will be able to visualise yourself doing it. Read the daily papers as often as you can, because reading the daily papers encourages you to become worldlier, which is an indispensable broadcasting skill; it also helps to expand vocabulary and learn how stories and views are articulated. Engrossing yourself in current news and all forms of speech radio not only creates a gratifying awareness of how the world turns but also makes you a better broadcaster.

If speech presentation inspires you, there are a number of things you can do to pursue this avenue. You could volunteer as a reporter for your local public service station or perhaps contact your local breakfast show team and offer to be a regular caller for their show (they always need callers). You could also get involved in student, Internet or community radio as a volunteer. In fact, applying for anything that will eventually get you near a microphone will be useful.

If you are feeling especially creative, you could even consider launching your own podcast series. If you cannot find an opening at a radio station, why not create one? At first, you could distribute your podcasts amongst close friends. If this goes well and you are brave, you could also post them to your social network and see what happens. If you have access to a microphone (we will discuss this later) you could even start to record email voice messages for your friends. This can be a lot of fun.

YouTube is another outlet; you could review movies, discuss current affairs or share your opinions and thoughts with the world. You will soon learn what content works and what doesn't. Sure, it's not radio presenting, but it is a form of speech presentation and it will vastly develop your experience and personality; it is always better to do something that points toward a goal than nothing at all! If you did decide to publish something, you might even gain a following, and that could launch your career.

Speech presentation is probably the most valuable skill when it comes to radio broadcasting and this is why we have covered it first. Gaining experience in speaking without music is worth its weight in gold. When you can excel at it, your job as a broadcaster will be an abundant one.

Commercial Radio Presentation

Obviously, commercial radio is driven by revenue. Remarkably, though, few presenters really understand or care, but they should. The business of commercial radio is to sell advertising. The more listeners a station has, the more they can charge for their advertising. The more they charge for their advertising, the more money they make. The more money they make, the more they spend on marketing, brand development, talent, research…and so it goes on. Successful radio presenters have a good understanding of this cycle and the role they play in the commercial radio picture.

Playing music is often the primary focus of commercial radio. The age group or type of desired listener defines this music and how it is played. Most radio stations have the most listeners in the morning, which is why they invest the most money on their breakfast shows. Breakfast and drive time shows traditionally contribute the most toward a station's audience because there are more available listeners at these times of the day than at others. Of course, all hours of the day are important, and there are some shows at different times that deliver listeners—some have even been known to out-perform breakfast and drive time, but these instances are rare.

Breakfast shows attract listeners differently than at other times of the day. Breakfast radio often involves more speech, as the aim is to deliver compelling content to retain or build audience. Breakfast and drive time shows are said to signify the two most likely times a listener may listen to that radio. At both times it is important that the listener is not given a reason to re-tune. The ideal outcome for any station is that a listener hears the breakfast show on their commute to work, listens while they work, and listens on their way home. In fact, if radio had its way, a listener would listen at dinner, then at night, then in bed and even while they sleep. If you are observant, you will notice how stations alter their content for various times of the day to cleverly maximise a good saturation of listening hours. Times of the day in segments are referred to by radio as "day-parts."

With the exception of talk stations, commercial radio presenters are required to have a passion for music. A presenter who can express a passion for the music played by a station is highly regarded.

Music stations might often make their sound uniform where possible. They conduct extensive research on habits, trends and tastes of their audience demographic and use this data to create a consistent sound and develop their brand. In any business, any product going to market has to have a strong brand in order to survive, and the business of radio is no exception. Understanding each station's brand is important, and we will discuss this in detail.

Some stations focus on being different, some focus on playing lots of music and others focus on the variety of personalities or content they offer. If you listen very carefully to radio stations, you will note that they all have a certain approach to everything they do. This is sometimes referred to as a "Style Guide." The Style Guide represents the music played, the things the presenters talk about and how the radio station positions itself to the market. The more you absorb each station's Style Guide, the greater your likelihood of success, because you will be able to tailor your content and approach depending on which commercial station you are aiming for.

Public service presentation

Public service presenters share many similarities to speech presenters and due to the nature of how public service stations operate, presenters tend to be older and more experienced. Younger presenters can still be found on specialist shows or national stations that attract youth audiences.

Just to be clear, the Wikipedia definition of public service radio states: "Public broadcasting includes radio, television and other electronic media outlets whose primary mission is public service. Public broadcasters receive funding from diverse sources including license fees, individual contributions, public financing and commercial financing." In most countries, public broadcasting operates both locally, regionally or nationally. Where commercial radio stations are bound by some limitations of being financed by advertising, public service stations are bound by the requirements of their licence.

In the UK, a large number of local and national public service presenters started their careers as journalists. Journalism skills are advantageous due to the style of broadcasting, but those without them can still become presenters.

On local stations, a large proportion of their focus is the local community and its news. Therefore, it pays for presenters to be passionate about their local area. If you are not able to develop an interest in your community, things might be more difficult.

There are three common industry speculations about public service stations. The first is that they are regarded as a closed shop. The second is that those who get in tend to stay in. Although we treat both of these speculations with a pinch of salt, industry professionals do observe a clear distinction between public service presenters and commercial presenters. They not only sound different, but they also have different goals and outlooks; this is very important to note. The third speculation is that public service stations like to source talent from within the organisation: talent that understands their programming ethos. This could be another reason why the aforementioned experience in different areas is useful.

In recent years, however, local stations have been employing more commercially-trained presenters—particularly those with more experience. Some say this is because commercial radio presenters are accustomed to a certain level of discipline that public service presenters are not typically required to develop. Regardless of whom they employ, public service stations have primary aims, which are completely different to those of commercial radio. Yes, they might be competing for the same listener, but they are also playing a very different game. Understanding this game will be your challenge, as we will describe in detail later.

Right now, local public service stations place a significant emphasis on the community, its people and its issues, so if you were keen to work at one, it might be useful to focus heavily on this in your application. Rather than sending a standardised demo, you might choose to produce and present an audio feature about the community and use that as a demo. If nothing else, your local passion, vision and creativity will be noted, and that might be all you need.

For the purposes of this book and to gain further insight into the workings of public service radio in general, we interviewed two former national presenters and a number of executive producers. We also interviewed key regional managers of local and regional stations to gain clues that might explain how people become successful or how people get to work on a national public service station.

One thing we noticed in terms of the national stations was how few public service presenters seem to be actually fulfilling lifelong ambitions. In other words, although they found themselves working on the biggest radio station in England, some of them don't or didn't view it as such a big deal. Very few individuals devoted their entire careers to reaching this level.

One presenter did. He told us how he would be stay up late every night visualising his goal of working at the UK's biggest station. He relayed just how much it had always meant to him and how many times he was rejected. Sheer determination and applied talent appeared to be the guiding force in his journey. It worked and he made it, although he does joke that when he finally succeeded, it had taken him so long that he was almost too old.

Another presenter, who soon became a household name, took a different route. He told us how his only focus in life was to be the best he could be at any one time. He succeeded by creating such a buzz about his work that the biggest station in the UK found it harder to ignore him. This wasn't the only time someone made it using this philosophy; in fact if you study the careers of many successful broadcasters today, you will see most of them have followed a similar path. It seems there is a good argument for just focusing on what you are doing now and pursuing current success in order to achieve future goals.

It was becoming clear, as we collated our findings, that the organisation behind these large national stations can be an unpredictable organism. To us, not one single route determined anyone's success, nor a particular set of skills or experience. It was often a combination of everything or nothing. One pattern, however, was becoming clear. When presenters were ready, provided they were suitable, they just seemed to find themselves there! It was either that the organisation found them or the opportunities required presented themselves naturally. The great Buddhist proverb sums this up perfectly: "When the student is ready, the teacher will appear."

Specialist presentation

The specialist presenter is an expert in a specific musical niche: dance, hip-hop or jazz, for example. There are lots of radio stations that carry specialist programmes, and there are even more specialist stations.

In this arena, the focus of presentation is on knowledge or adoration of the genre rather than on specific industry techniques. Presenters of specialist programmes live a lifestyle in keeping with their niche and are rather more passionate about being around the music than they are about being on the radio. That in itself is a powerful clue regarding success. In an interview with a well-known, national radio producer, we learned how presenters on his station all unconditionally live and breathe the lifestyle of the music they play. He told us that the people they are looking for on that station don't just know and love the music, but they are as obsessive and fanatical as its followers.

The culture of specialist programming is more relaxed, and if you have genuine talent and a love for your niche, you might find it comparatively easy to get started. Some presenters in mainstream radio today actually started their careers as specialist presenters. They may have presented a dance show on a commercial station or a jazz show on a local public service station, for example. Other presenters have cultivated an entire career following and presenting their single niche. The only caveat is that specialist programming pays little or nothing until you reach the big time.

The good news is, because specialist stations have little or no rules, your technique and experience is almost immaterial. There are no Style Guides or formats, very few restrictions due to licences or revenues and very little pressure in the environment. Solar Radio in London is a great example to reference—none of the presenters have a uniformed style or technique, but all of them sound great. This is because they are all simply doing what they love and talking about what they know. While some might find it difficult to work in mainstream radio without rethinking what they do, they probably don't want to. Listening to how these presenters enthuse about music is fascinating and in many ways can offer commercial radio presenters inspiration on the concept of music passion.

If you wanted to head in this direction, you could start by making contact with your favourite niche stations.

If you are that fanatical and there is a unique audience for your music, you could even start broadcasting to your niche yourself—some people record podcasts or even get involved in setting up their own specialist stations on the Internet. Existing Internet stations are an excellent platform for gaining experience too. They run on tight budgets, so if you were to offer to record some "links" (bits where you talk) for them or do a slot for free, you might get lucky. Start by making a list of all the stations that play your favourite music on Tunein.com and get in contact with the producers or management.

Now that we've explored the different types of radio presenters, let's take a look at the way in which you would begin your career as any one of these. Regardless of what type you want to become, you are going to need a demo. Demos are the most important part of your radio broadcasting journey.

Making a Demo

A demo is the only chance you get to make an impression. It will always be the currency by which you trade. The power of the demo cannot be emphasised enough. Regardless of how good or bad a presenter is, it's all about their demo. The content, the length, the order and the tone are all equally important elements. A demo can make the best presenter sound awful and the worst presenter sound great.

Starting with length, we often cause controversy with our opinion, but for music radio, we recommend a demo to be no longer than 90 seconds. For speech heavy or breakfast radio a demo should be no more than 3 minutes.

We recommend these lengths for two reasons. The first is because programme controllers or editors simply don't have time to listen all the way through to every demo they receive. The second is because management instinctively know in a matter of seconds if a presenter's sound and style is what they are looking for.

Demos are always going to be limiting. Some presenters feel demos are quite unfair, and they are absolutely right. While demos and their limitations are unfair, they are an essential aspect of the business. We still debate demo length with all types and levels of presenters and management, but we always remind people—if 90 seconds is the average length of a theatrical trailer, why should a radio demo be longer?

The following strategies will improve your success rate, not just for creating a good demo, but also for being a successful presenter. It is therefore important to absorb the following principals until they become second nature. If you already have presenting experience or have a demo, this is a good opportunity for you to appraise what you have been doing. If you have never done a demo before, using these principals will immediately give your demo that polished edge.

Among the many principals in radio presenting, the following four components are the most important when starting out or making a demo:

1.Targeting

2.Acting

3.Brevity

4.Content

Targeting

Targeting is by far the most important of the four ideas. Targeting means being extremely focused on where you want to go and what you want to achieve, before setting out to achieve it. Targeting also refers to the type of content you choose to put on each demo or how you construct content for broadcast.

Just as you would tailor your CV and cover letter to each prospective employer, so should you tailor your

demo. It is unlikely that just one demo will always be enough because many stations do things differently from one another.

Many years ago, demos consisted of a selection of the presenter's best links. Nowadays, the more successful demos are those that are correctly targeted to a particular station or programme. It seems obvious, but even seasoned professionals ignore this essential fact. Granted, if you have valuable material such as previous shows, excellent previously recorded content, a winning moment on air or a really good link, use it, but it should rarely substitute the ideas we discuss here.

The principal of targeting is simple. Decide which station or type of station you want to work on, learn and master their Style Guide and reflect this knowledge and appreciation in your demo. It really is as simple as that. Doing a demo any other way is categorically unproductive. Showing a station you unequivocally understand their Style Guide is an absolute must: the number one rule.

In order to perfect targeting in your demo, the first step is to absorb as much of the content on your target station as possible. If you really want to absorb it, you can record and listen to a typical hour or two a number of times so you can study the following:

1. The types of things the presenters are talking about

2. The average length of time the presenters speak for

3. The presenters' tone and speed

4. The sorts of phrases they use

5. The overall station message or idea

If you are able to demonstrate knowledge of the above, your demo will outclass many others. If, in your demo, you are sounding similar, using similar content, as well as similar music, length of time speaking and tone, you will already be ten times more likely to make the right impact than others.

For breakfast radio, your goal is to be unique, but you still need to display an understanding of the audience. It's no use having a brilliant demo if all your content is aimed at the wrong age group, for example.

Regardless of the type of radio station, all on-air content is always carefully targeted. Stations evaluate material by referring to it as either "on target" or "not target." Some say "on brand" or "off brand." Your demo, then, must be on target and on brand.

Using the station's name doesn't count as correct targeting; you still can do a targeted demo without using the station's name. It might be advisable, if you were considering making something bespoke, to ask permission to use the station name. If you have access to jingles or imaging, on no account should you ever use that on a demo. We think this is categorically discourteous and may result in immediate disqualification.

The more closely you understand a station and everything that is happening on air, the better you will sound. Do not cut corners; you have to sound like you already work there as much as possible.

Because of this, only ever use the same type of content on your demo that you might hear on the target station and make it perfectly accurate. One good editing exercise when writing or creating your links is to imagine yourself writing content for one of the station's existing presenters to read!

Case Study: In a targeting experiment, we worked with a presenter who had not been successful applying for a job at a certain radio station. He was frustrated and so he came to us. We listened to his demo and noted that it sounded nothing like the station he was approaching.

As the presenter was clearly confused as to what a correct demo entailed and how to correct his current demo, we asked him to record two hours of the radio station and transcribe all the presenter links. We then taught the presenter the differences between his and the station's content and illustrated where he was going wrong. In particular, we explained how none of his original content matched that of his target station. His speed and tone was different, as were the subjects he spoke of, and how he approached them. He used terminology that seemed out of place with his target station and he missed out some fundamental key principals, which we will explore later.

Once he understood these distinctions, we asked him to alter the transcribed content and try re-recording his demo using that as an experiment. The resulting demo sounded completely different. It was so different that the presenter received a very glowing response from the original programme controller. Ultimately the presenter illustrated to the programmed controller his understanding of the radio station. He has now greatly increased his chances of getting on air at his target station.

Acting

If you are a stand-up comedian, actor, mobile DJ or a brilliant public speaker, this section might not apply to you, because a form of acting is inherently natural as part of your job. You will have a mode that you adopt just before you perform. If, however, you are like most people, you will need to develop some acting skills to make life easier for you at the outset of your broadcasting career. Acting and developing a persona will alleviate nerves and help you greatly.

When coaching presenters, radio management use words like, natural, relaxed, real, passionate and genuine. When you start out, you will likely feel none of these things on the radio. This is why we like to encourage you to "fake it till you make it." Develop a character, if you will.

One way to create your character at first is to emulate or model your favourite presenters. You can borrow some of their techniques before you find your own. This is not to suggest, of course, that you try to sound like anyone, but rather learn how they articulate themselves and adopt one or two content formulation ideas from them. This is a form of modelling, not copying. Modelling is used in Nuero Linguistic Programming or NLP and is the process of adopting the behaviours, language, strategies and beliefs of another person in order to build a model of what they do and work towards similar outcomes.

Just like learning to drive a car, this process will feel peculiar at first but soon will become an unconscious skill. The more practice you get, the faster you can start to invent your own techniques that will gradually replace those you borrowed.

Another useful tip is to imagine stepping out of your skin and into a person who is already very experienced. Adopt the same mind-set as this professional broadcaster and act accordingly. This is a form of creative visualisation, which can be useful in everything you do. Creative visualisation is also used by some of the greatest sportsmen in the world; footballers have to first visualise the ball going in the net before being able to do it for real. In your case, you just need to visualise a confident, experienced presenter. Before long you will sound like one.

One of the industry's current bugbears is the concept of the "DJ voice," that unusual voice a person adopts the moment they put on headphones! It's hard to accept at first, but however bad you think your real voice sounds, it will always sound better than a false one. Discovering how to be comfortable talking normally near a microphone and understanding that this authenticity actually creates a deeper, wider and more interesting sound than anything else is nothing short of a breakthrough.

Women tend to put on deeper voices in an attempt to sound more professional or less squeaky, and men usually put on voices they think will sound better on the radio—perhaps more dynamic or butch. The results of these manipulations are counterproductive. As you will learn later in our microphone section, the broadcast microphone amplifies a voice in a unique manner; it picks up everything that is naturally there and adds texture to it. Add this to an "EQ chain" and "Optimod" (explained later), and a natural voice sounds quite wonderful all by itself. Restricting the natural tones of a voice in any way simply gets magnified when it goes to air. We have tried to explain countless times to people how nice it is to hear a person talking on the radio in their normal voice. This is because, as listeners, we identify more when something sounds genuine. If you don't like the sound of your voice, understand that it is already beautiful, and you don't need to do anything more to it, other than become more comfortable with the way it naturally sounds.

Because it is hard to identify when you're putting on a voice, one-way to test it is to practice links, with and without headphones and note the difference.

Example 1: A radio boss once insisted that one of his breakfast show presenters never used headphones during his show. He liked the presenter's articulation but thought his voice sounded too "DJ." The presenter was offended at first but now agrees that it was a worthwhile and valuable exercise. He eventually agreed with his boss that he sounded more like a normal person without headphones. This is your goal too.

Example 2: Another presenter in his early career decided to develop a "laid back" element to his character in an attempt to sound proficient and relaxed. While it sounded relaxed to him, he was actually told he sounded bored, sleepy and intoxicated! It was not until quite late in his career when a producer made him force a grin before talking that he was able to notice the difference and make a change.

Radio management will encourage presenters to speak as though they were addressing a friend. This is good advice, and although you might not always be talking about the same type of things as you would with a friend, their intention is to help you to use similar tonality and intention so that you sound natural and genuine.

Brevity

Brevity is a formidable skill to cultivate. It means using the fewest number of words to get a message across. It is easy to fall into the trap where you think that the more you say, the better of a speaker you are. In fact, the opposite is true. Presenters always have a certain allocated time for speech, even on talk radio, and so your goal is to learn to use language smartly.

Learning to use less words to say the same thing will not only help you in radio, but in all aspects of your life. Mastering brevity can also improve your negotiation skills and your relationships with people. It doesn't mean being blunt—it just means choosing words carefully and keeping things succinct.

To give you an example in music radio, in the 1990s, there were several studies published both academically and by private companies that tracked the attention spans of listeners when presenters were talking. The studies revealed that listeners to music radio start to lose interest the moment presenters begin to talk. Although it was an exhaustive study, one of the overall findings showed that a listener's attention span started to diminish after only three to five seconds of a presenter's link. This is one of the reasons why brevity is key in radio.

Many years later, a rival company advanced the findings of these studies and created a simple but effective technique for its breakfast shows. While the technique had a specific name we will call it a "Power link."

A Power Link referred to the concept of making an influential or powerful statement at the beginning of a presenter link. It was believed to encourage listeners to pay attention at the beginning of links and thus stay interested for longer. For example, a presenter might start a sentence with, "All women can't drive," and then continue substantiating the idea. The theory was to captivate listeners beyond the above-mentioned 3 – 5 seconds.

For about a year the company encouraged all their breakfast shows to devise and include Power Links every day. In theory, the idea was practical; however, in application it failed and was later dropped. It was dropped for several reasons. Firstly, the audience could have sensed they were being manipulated. Secondly, shows that could not quite master the technique sounded contrived, and thirdly, the company noted the technique was not congruent with their intention to sound real. Regardless of its failure, the technique still illustrates the immense value in finding ways to pique interest as long as they come across as genuine.

Back to brevity: overall, one clear benefit of mastering it at the beginning of your career is that it will save you from making mistakes, both on air and on a demo.

Example - When one of the authors of this book started in radio, his programme controller only permitted him to go on air provided he spoke in 10-second segments. While initially confused, he soon learned that 10 seconds is plenty of time in music radio, especially when consumed with nerves.

Meetings were scheduled where the programme controller would sit down with the presenter and listen to his shows, and he would use a stopwatch to monitor the length of the presenter's links. In these meetings (often called snoops), the programme controller explained that if a person can say, "I love you" or "I want a divorce" in 2 or 3 seconds, 10 seconds is plenty of time for any link.

This example is one great way of explaining brevity, but you can see it in application every day. A 2-hour movie only has 10-90 seconds in a trailer to make you want to see it. A billboard advertisement has 2 seconds to illustrate why you want a product, and web designers have 50 milliseconds to make a good first impression online.

Learn to think vigilantly about the smartest way you can get a message across. Each link you are proposing to put on air or on a demo should first be planned with brevity in mind. You simply will not be able to work in music radio if you do not understand, practice and employ this principle. Sending short emails and writing good tweets are excellent practice, and while you might not choose speak in 140 characters on the radio, could you?

In music radio, outside of breakfast, it is often said that if any of your links are more than 10 or 20 seconds, they need to be tremendously entertaining or they should be abandoned. Certainly, this rule applies when making a great demo. Knowing that radio companies all over the world have spent millions on research and training just to teach you why it's important to say less is of immense value to you. Ignore this advice at your peril!

The notion of a listener attention span is quite a useful when you are new on the radio. Largely in music radio, the listener is rarely hanging on to your every word; believe it or not, this is a good thing. You would be surprised how little the listener notices even when you make a mistake. This is why presenters rarely correct their mistakes, as it sounds bad pointing one out when the listener may not have noticed. Knowing the listeners aren't waiting to laugh at you when you make a mistake helps with nerves.

There are times when you do need to captivate. There are times when what you say can create an emotional reaction from a listener. There are times you might make a listener laugh out loud, burst into tears, want to call you, want to participate in your show, want to dance or want to tell all their friends about you. There will be times when listeners will want to sit in their car and wait for you to finish what you are saying. They will shout at the radio, tweet about you, text about you...and the list goes on. All these things will happen after first mastering the art of brevity.

Content

Content is the fabric of presentation. It is what creates uniqueness and, as a result, generates and retains audience. Content is the thing that makes a movie live up to its trailer, it is what you choose to write in a greetings card to someone, the difference between a good book and bad one and the reason why someone might switch their radio on or off. Content is what makes a person like you, it is how a letter or email makes you feel, it is those emotive words in a song. Content is what you and everyone else identifies with. This is why they say content is king.

Content is made up of two elements. The first is what you say; the second is how you say it. In their books, authors James Borg and Michael Gladwell both explore how we as humans communicate. Borg's findings in his book Influence show that only 7% of normal communication is verbal, and the rest is nonverbal. Blink, by Malcolm Gladwell, investigates how humans learn a great deal from each other purely through an instinctive manner. Essentially, Gladwell demonstrates that "there can be as much in the blink of an eye as in months of rational analysis." What these and many other findings tell us is that communication can often be more about how we say something than what we say.

When radio management teach the delivery of content, they use words and phrases like "warmth," "smile in the voice," "conviction," "upbeat," "bright," "passionate" and so on to coach their presenters. They might also use the expressions, "say it like you mean it" or "make it your own." All of these phrases are useful. What radio stations are trying to encourage with these terms and phrases is more of that "real-ness" we discussed earlier. As you become a more experienced broadcaster, you will be able to radiate all of these things on air, but it starts with developing an intention and mind-set of authenticity in order to learn to connect with your listener.

We are all very observant creatures—tiny hints of sadness can be detected in the undertones of our speech in the same way that joy can. Often what we feel can come across in our choice of words or our tonality, so it makes sense that if you are talking to many listeners you need to be in the right frame of mind and employ the right intention. This is one of the reasons why in entertainment they say to "leave your personal stuff at the door," which ties in with our description of the importance of adapting a character on air.

Ideally, your content and tonality should be born out of a sense of genuine cheerfulness and balance. See presenting like meeting a good friend for coffee. Being on the radio is the same.

Creating good radio or demo content is also based upon understanding the three words: compelling, relevant and relatable. In other words, is what you're about to say interesting enough to keep someone listening? Is what you are about to say relevant to the day, situation or context of the moment? And can the listener identify with what you are about to say?

In personality, speech or breakfast radio the above guidelines apply but there are other factors in play as well. Is it funny? Is it interesting enough? Is it unique? Will it create a reaction?

On radio stations that focus heavily on music you might add to this by asking yourself the following questions: Is what you are about to say about the music? Are you adding anything to the music? Are you selling the music? Are you helping the music flow? Are you sharing your passion?

Generally speaking, listeners tend to be apathetic and listen to the radio passively. Unless you give a listener a reason to care about you or the radio station, they probably won't. Your job is to make them care or, in other words, find ways to add value. What's in it for the listener?

Before speaking on the radio, first clearly picture a single person. Some presenters find it helpful to take a picture into the studio of their target listener. Imagine the listener to be an intelligent friend. And remember that initially, your only goal is just to encourage them to feel comfortable with you and the station.

One way to do this is to use content and delivery in accordance with how the listener might be feeling. The more you understand the target listener, the easier this will be. Most radio stations know their target listener inside out. They know their habits, their personalities, likes and dislikes...even what TV shows they watch. They will share this information with you, which will be of great help. For the purposes of your demo, though, you will have to do some research.

Making good content for a demo can be as simple as following some formulas. While every demo should ideally be targeted and a certain length, there are also fundamental dos and don'ts that will improve the end result. Exploring these will not only help you make better demos, but also help speed up your success on the whole. Rather than calling them dos and don'ts, though, we will call them cautions and recommendations. It sounds nicer, and it's always good to find better ways to say things—another tip perhaps?

Cautions

Be careful of expressing strong opinions on demos or on air, as the listener may disagree with you. Especially early in your career, this is the last thing you want.

Get some basic legal knowledge so you can express yourself without inadvertently vilifying someone.

There is an entire book on what you can and cannot say on the radio. It is called "Hang the DJ" and can be purchased from radiobookshop.com.

Be conscious of the length of your links. For music radio, if they are longer than 10-20 seconds each, they might be too long.

If you do a news-based story, you don't always need to cite a reference or source. The listener trusts that what you are saying is a fact and that you are the one bringing them the news. It sounds better to own the content, unless of course it's someone else's material.

Be careful of listing a selection of things the listener might be doing. Some presenters do this in an attempt to be relatable. For example they might say, "You might be on the way to work, you might be in the shower, you might have some friends round, you might be getting ready to go out, etc." In actual fact, the listener might not be doing any of these things. If you pick just one, it sounds less contrived.

Watch out for clichés, as radio stations are really not keen on these. The bigger and more successful the radio station, the larger their emphasis is on avoiding them.

Always check to be sure that you are using language that is real in your demo. Make sure you speak how people speak in real life and as naturally as possible. Using phrases like "On your Monday," "Stick around" and "You can bag yourself" are not phrases in normal speech. Similarly, filler words such as "currently," "right now" and "of course" are terms to be avoided or replaced with something better. We all know that radio is not a natural environment and that the notion of speaking in real language is somewhat a contradiction, but on the whole, if you can at least keep an eye on what you're saying and how real it comes across, this insight will be helpful.

Know when to stay off the music. Try to respect the music as much as possible. Radio stations consider misuse of music very bad practice. In the past, one radio group even imposed a complete ban on presenters talking over music. The ban rigorously enforced presenters never to speak on more than a second of song. Transgressors were considered insubordinate.

Some radio stations, on the other hand, use music intros as part of their overall sound. They do this to regulate pace and brevity. They encourage presenters to start songs before talking, so as to keep the station urgent and continuous. They also sometimes use clips of artists, callers, or station branding on intros.

The ends of songs are a different matter. These are to be respected the most. Songs which come to a natural end should be allowed to do so always. Songs that fade should be allowed space, before you start to talk on them.

As a general rule of thumb, in consideration of your demo, show different ways of using music to enhance or decorate your content. Research how your prospective station uses the music to be sure that your demo is keeping with their style. Some introductions of songs can add immense value to your delivery; they might add a sense of context, colour or tone, so look for opportunities. Anthemic song intros should be left alone, as should songs that are extremely significant. Sometimes the intro is the best bit—be careful not to spoil it. Simply talking up to vocals or talking all over the ends of songs will never impress a programme manager—what you say and how you say it will make the biggest impression.

Next, if you don't really believe something or you wouldn't say it to a friend, it's best not to say it on the radio. If you are about to make an observation, first imagine how you would phrase it to a friend. Really imagine your friend sitting there and imagine his or her face as you talk. Would they cringe?

Avoid spoiling a TV show or movie by giving away too much information. With TV on demand, presenters can no longer assume that everyone has seen a show at the time of its broadcast. Recommending something forthcoming is always better than saying "Did you see X last night?"

Never start talking until you know how you are going to stop. Some presenters early in their career write down their entire links to ensure that they don't wander off at a tangent. Others use a few keywords as reminders. It's amazing how blank your mind can go when the red light is on and you have already started speaking. Even real professionals know their "out" before they start.

Recommendations

Referring to yourself or your character can be very entertaining when it is done well. Having a unique observation or sharing your perspective can be utterly compelling. Many household name presenters and breakfast shows base their entire acts upon talking about their lives. The same applies to comedians. Some people are natural storytellers, others are less so, and only experience will guide you in this regard. Look on YouTube at your favourite comedy clips to see how comedians turn ordinary events into interesting stories. Listen to as many breakfast shows as possible and learn how they approach their content.

Test your content. If you have an observation on something or an idea, try posting it as a Facebook update, or Tweet it. If you get some "likes" or responses, it could be a sign you can create good broadcast content. You can also test your ideas with friends on the phone or over drinks. Even talking to strangers or engaging in small talk can help you understand how different people view the world and what is important to them. Listening to, observing or noticing how people speak to one another is also useful for learning to speak the "language of the listener."

As covered in the targeting section, always replicate the types of content that your target station is broadcasting in your demo. Talk about the same sorts of subjects as they do.

Highlight items that are happening on the radio station or the radio station's website. This is often called "selling the station." Many have retained high paying jobs and long careers by doing only that and nothing else!

In music radio, look for reasons **why** you are playing a particular song. Even though the radio station might have play-listed it for you, the listener still thinks you are choosing the songs. If you are going to say that you like a song, find a reason **why** you like it. This is sometimes referred to as "selling the music."

You can also elaborate on music by adding value to it. Adding value to music involves making the music more interesting. You can share information on a song, point out where the song might be used in a movie or TV show, illustrate what the song reminds you of or ask what the song might remind a listener of. What do the lyrics mean? What is the story behind the song?

Add a "sense of day" as often as possible. This means always knowing when it's "back to school day," "bank holiday," "end of semester" and so on. What are your listeners thinking? What might they be planning? How can your material reflect a sense that you know what is going on in their lives? How they might be feeling? Are you in the same position as them? Most of the time what you are thinking is much the same as what the listener is thinking, so experiment. Are you tired of too much rain? Did you get stuck in the same road-works? Are you attending the same event as they are?

Promote one or two songs that are coming up and find an interesting way to do so. In speech or breakfast radio you could promote a feature in the same way. In radio, this is called "teasing." Whenever you hear a presenter "throw forward" to something in the future, this is a tease. In commercial radio and television, teasing is used to carry a listener through a break. This is why in TV shows, there is often a cliff hanger or crucial moment just before the commercials.

Creating good teases is something you will be required to do, so include some in your demo. A whole book could be written on teasing ideas alone, but for now, try to think of an interesting, cryptic or unique way to "forward sell" something. If you listen carefully enough, you will hear some great examples that you can learn from or borrow.

Refer to social media in your demo. Radio stations have Twitter and Facebook pages and they read out tweets, texts and emails. Some producers even make up this content to help guide the listener in the right participation direction. You can do this too. What is trending in social networks? Can you cleverly make this **your own** observation or refer to it?

Using callers in demos is one extremely important element, and if you have the capacity to include them, they should be introduced very early on in your demo. Conversations with callers should be just that— conversations. Rather than asking a series of questions and getting "yes" or "no" answers, you should focus your attention on asking questions that encourage callers to speak more than you.

Using what, when, why and how questions evoke more than a "yes" or "no" response and can save you from embarrassing silences. Even though most radio stations record calls, you can still use this interview technique pre-record.

A great tip is to interview the caller first to find something interesting about them before putting them on air. Public service stations have producers who do this for the presenter and as a result, normally sound better. When you have some good information before taking a call to air, you have an idea as to the direction of the call and where you want to end it before you start. Try being an investigator of information, and you will be sure to find something juicy. By interviewing a caller before going on air, you are gauging their responses and rehearsing the call at the same time—this puts both you and the caller at ease. Having found out something about the caller, you can use that to start the conversation, for example, "John has been spending most of his weekend standing half way up a ladder. How have you managed that, John?"

Callers are also a brilliant way to gauge your ability to sound natural. The more natural you sound and conversational you are, the better the caller will respond to you. If you "DJ voice" all over them and try and make jokes, they will respond in a clipped or guarded fashion. We have all heard presenters try to engage in conversation with a listener, and it sound uncomfortable. Make the caller your friend before putting them on your show but be sure to make it sound genuine.

To elaborate on this point, the editor of this book was once called by a radio station at 7 a.m. with the good news she had won a prize. During the on air call the presenter was trying so hard to be an "enthusiastic breakfast DJ" that he didn't account for the fact that she had barely woken up and didn't speak to her accordingly. The resulting call sounded embarrassing for all concerned. While she was genuinely grateful to win and was happy to chat on the radio, she was so taken aback by being thrust on the radio and by the presenter's overly bouncy personality that he was only able to respond with one-word answers. While the presenter might have elucidated that she was a bad caller, in reality her performance was his responsibility. There are very few excuses for putting a bad caller to air.

In closing this section, the above few recommendations really can apply for almost every demo you create and although speech, specialist or BBC stations all have different styles, these guidelines cover the most important basics of presentation at a professional level. Use them well and you will be walking on-air in no time.

Editing a demo

Later in the book we will take a look at the ways in which you can record and edit your demo. Firstly though, this section here covers the order and sequence of the ideal demo.

If the primary goal of sending out your demo is getting someone to listen to it, then the second aim should be to get him or her to listen to all of it. In order to achieve that, consider three important elements: length, order and content.

Length

A radio demo should be ideally no longer than 90 seconds or 2 minutes for radio that covers more speech. 3 – 5 minutes for public service radio is acceptable. Less is always more.

Order

Choosing the right order of content is more important than it might seem. Great presenters are all too often unfairly represented by what they choose to put on their demos.

The general rule of thumb is that the shortest links should always go at the front of the demo. The strongest content should also be at the front. It's even better if your strongest content also happens to be short.

Content

Obviously a demo only contains links, and therefore there should only be very short clips of the music you use. In speech radio there might not be any music at all.

Some people edit their demos tightly so there is only a millisecond between the end of one link and the beginning of another. Others choose to slowly fade the music or content between each link, which can allow the listener to absorb what they are hearing. Either or both work as well as the other. The more adult-oriented your target station, the slower the flow of your demo can be; again, follow the target station's rhythm and pace.

Music radio stations love callers as well as your relationship with the music. If you can include an interaction with a caller or more than one caller, this should definitely be included, but again unless you can find a unique reason for the caller being there, leave it out. Some presenters ask friends to call them for the purposes of their demo, try to avoid this as it rarely sounds genuine.

Speech radio might listen for the way you articulate, your conversational approach and the content you have chosen. They will be looking for indications of your research, knowledge of your topics, or your perspective on a piece. Originality is favoured here.

Specialist radio stations like to hear your passion and knowledge for the music or its scene and prefer content to be centred on the music rather than your personality.

The whole purpose of each piece of content in your demo is to encourage the listener to continue listening. You can be ingenious as to how you do this. Movies sometimes start midway through an action scene or with a strong piece of narrative. When approaching your demo think in the same way as a movie editor, and like a movie, demos are best when they include a story, theme, structure or pattern.

Some of the best demos we have come across have been constructed in such a unique way that we are compelled to listen. They might open mid-way through a crucial moment on air, such as a competition or the sound of a phone ringing. Some presenters have opened demos with their studio team laughing; others just sound great because of how the presenter sounds alongside a piece of music. Look for ways where you can create an opening to your demo that might make someone engaged or intrigued. Remember, the first 10 seconds are crucial and can make or break your demo.

Public service radio stations, on the whole, love to hear interviews. Setting up or promoting an interview in your demo would be useful, as would actually conducting one. Certainly, this will affect the length of your demo, but in this case, an exception can be made. If you do decide to record an interview with someone, remember that your questions and the first few seconds of each answer are all that the programme controller needs to hear—you can fade out the rest.

If you can pick a subject relevant to the local community and conduct an interview about that, again, this could be highly valuable. Correspondingly, if you can to acquire "vox pops" (short clip, recordings from the general public) about a local topic and add these to your demo, your efforts might be surprisingly rewarding. Imagine writing to a programme controller or editor saying...

Dear Name,

In my enclosed presenter demo for your consideration, I have taken the liberty to include members of the local community speaking on the subject of the planned building works in the city centre.

Although I would like to express an interest in joining your team, I would also welcome your feedback on my handling of this subject or any other material in the demo.

Your thoughts would greatly help me formulate a better understanding of ABC FM, and I would really appreciate your time and expertise.

Yours sincerely,

Your name

Contact telephone

Link to your Radio Talent page, Website or demo.

By far, the most effective demo construction method is to replicate a typical hour of your target station. This means identifying and including similar types of links and content. On music stations, for example, a typical hour's content might be categorised as follows:

1.A short speed link (a very short link that simply identifies the station and introduces or promotes forthcoming music).

2. A music link (a link that is about the music).

3. A personality link (a link that has some element of personality or "sense of the day" in it).

4. A station-based link (a link that identifies activity on or around the station).

5.A forward sell or tease (a link which includes a tease or the unique promotion of something).

6. A competition execution (a link which shows your ability to explain or solicit an on air competition).

7.An interaction link (a link interacting with a third party).

In the targeting section, we explored how you might identify the types of content being used on the station, but largely, at the time of writing, 80% of all music radio stations follow the above parameters in each hour outside of breakfast.

While this, then, is very sensible demo planning, you can also choose to completely ignore it and do your own thing. If the idea of formulas and templates makes your toes curl, you can simply throw them all out the window and rely on your personality.

Some of the best presenters in the world have absolutely no templates, guides, or structure to their acts and refuse to follow any station formats. What they do have is an inimitable natural flair for being fascinating when they speak. Others are so accomplished in the basics that they can deliver content to sound deliberately ad hoc and unprepared. It can all work. The above guidelines are simply suggestions for the start of your career to minimise errors that could stand in your way. If you prefer to record a single piece of dialogue of just you talking, this might be all you need to start a life-changing career; there is always more than one way of doing something. This book is merely to inspire you to choose a direction that empowers and excites you.

Horses for courses. If you want to be a zany breakfast show host, take all the above with a pinch of salt.

Creativity

Do not be disheartened with the concept that radio is a business or ideas like brevity. While these are extremely important, it is easy to see them as negative, perhaps elements that stifle creativity and expression, but this is not the case.

We refer to things like brevity and the importance of targeting purely to get you to your most effective starting point. Once you have your foot in the door and proved yourself, there are an abundance of ways you can be creative and have fun. No radio station parameters or formats ever really stifle presenters; they simply challenge them to think more. This is what makes the game more interesting. A viewpoint, an opinion or a unique personality is valuable, but a basic understanding of radio station requirements is mandatory. If you want to move into the professional leagues, understanding a few codes of practice will help you. Big time radio is not a playground, and it is much better that you are forewarned at this point in your career rather than develop an amazing set of skills that are superfluous. Having the backing from your broadcaster to share creativity is much more beneficial when it is a team effort.

Radio is a constantly evolving media. There is increasing pressure on radio stations to deliver content that is compelling. As more and more methods of consuming media are invented, radio has a progressively difficult task of winning a share of listeners' daily attention. Radio has to invest considerably in researching listener personalities and habits and it has to absorb and study all forms of competing media in order to know how to adapt, evolve and survive. Creativity is therefore radio's best friend, and as a result, the role of presenting will always change and will always require vast amounts of creativity and forward thinking.

One minute, you will be required to be funny and the next minute, serious. One minute you will be required to make a daily script entertaining. The next minute you might be executing a competition. Develop a sense of trust that radio knows just what to do in order to be creative enough to retain and gain an audience and then enjoy the journey.

Presenter Courses

On radio training courses, presenters pay a fee to learn the basics of being on the radio. The great thing about presenter courses is that your demo is normally included in the price. The course tutors will also help you with your order, content and recording.

Presenter courses for people with no experience can be nerve racking, so choosing the course that makes you feel the most comfortable is important. If you are not 100% comfortable, your nerves might spoil how your demo sounds in the end. Conversely, natural performers and fast learners can attend a course and be working on a radio station months later. Your relationship with the tutors and the surroundings play a significant role.

Most of the courses take place in authentic studio environments where you will be taught how music is played on air using "play-out systems" and learn the basics of the broadcast desk, or the "board" as it is called in the US and Canada. The tutor will be able to quickly identify your strengths and help you with your content, which can save you a lot of time. The courses will also give you an insight into the workings of radio and the structure of radio programming.

The following media courses were happy for us to promote them in this book. In no particular order, we recommend you approach the following companies. Prices and details are subject to change.

Dynamic Media Academy
(www.dynamicmediaaccademy.com)

These courses are hosted in an authentic radio station environment and operated by Scott Myers, producer of a large popular breakfast show in the North of the UK. Andi Durrant, an esteemed networked presenter and Nick Riley a high profile specialist producer, are also connected with the operation.

The prices of the courses start at £295. This includes getting key contacts, personal career advice and a demo.

Yellow Media (www.yellow-media.co.uk)

Hosted from their own purpose built studios, these courses are run by ex-presenter Chris Brooks, who has hosted programmes on some of the UK's most prestigious commercial radio stations.

The prices of the courses start from £199. This includes a finished demo.

Radio City Academy (www.radiocityacademy.com)

Again hosted on location at various radio stations around the North of England and run by the founders of the National Broadcasting School. This company is offering a host of other courses including journalism, which is useful for public service broadcasting. Prices start from £149 for a typical weekend course.

Media School (www.media-courses.com)

A London-based academy with vast experience covering all types of media courses from make-up, acting, documentary filmmaking, photography, TV presenting, camera lighting, radio presenting and more.

Courses start at £175, which includes the creation of your demo. Example course times might be 11 a.m. till 5 p.m. They also offer intensive 5-day courses that include a demo for £749.

All these courses have first-rate track records, are an excellent solution and are more cost-effective than hiring your own studio. However, if you prefer to and have the resources, you could also enquire about one-on-one training or studio time with them. This is something we also recommend.

When choosing a course, keep targeting in mind. The tutors you choose must be on your wavelength and have expertise in the right area. Here are some useful points for consideration:

1. How long might you get in the studio?

2. What will you learn in their syllabus and how relevant is it to your goal?

3. Are there any finished demo products you can listen to before you book?

4. Are there any success stories they can share?

5. Do they offer studio hire and personal instruction?

6. What play-out system do they use?

Years ago some radio presenter schools were frowned upon by the radio industry. The schools started creating demos for presenters in a formulaic way, so much so that radio stations were able to tell which course a presenter had attended just by listening to their demo. This didn't do the presenter any favours. Some courses became synonymous for producing below-par demos. Either they did not reflect what was happening on the radio at the time or their candidates were sent out into the world with false hopes. This has all changed today, and radio-training companies have a more honest approach and manage their students' expectations realistically. They are also run by high-profile industry folk who are passionate about creating new talent and sustaining the industry.

Aside from taking courses, there are other ways to create demos, as we have previously mentioned. Be creative, start emailing producers or presenters on Radio Talent (www.radiotalent.co.uk) and look on LinkedIn. They sometimes have access to studios that you can borrow or rent. They might also be able to produce demos for you for a fee. Talk to colleges and universities, community stations, Internet stations and hospital radio stations—they might be willing to hire out their studio with or without an engineer.

You could talk to other presenters, established or otherwise, and ask them how they created their demos in the beginning. You might even get lucky and find a presenter who might tutor or help you. You might even, with a little creativity, set up your own studio at home. This way, you can practice over and over again. If no one will give you a slot where you can practice, create your own.

Creating a Studio

Just as the accessibility of specialist equipment had an impact in the world of the DJ, so to has it for broadcasting. Just as the DJ was able to buy a mixer and some decks from a store and practice mixing, so too can a presenter broadcast or record at home. Many years ago, a home studio was a luxury.

Nowadays, the home studio market has created an industry of its own. There are even some presenters who do shows on very big radio stations from their houses.

It doesn't need to be a daunting task nor does it need to cost a small fortune. You can be set up in no time, creating podcasts, recording content for radio stations abroad, recording demos, learning editing and so on. Once you have a facility of your own, you will be amazed at how the equipment can become useful in so many other ways too.

While you can really go town, you can get by with just a microphone, some headphones, a mixer, two cd players, a computer with speakers and some editing software. To break it down, you can follow these five steps:

Step One: The Mic

We have used two companies that specialise in microphones: The Mic Store (www.themicstore.co.uk) and A to Z Mics (www.atozmics.co.uk). You could contact them and ask them to recommend an entry-level broadcast microphone and stand.

Broadcast microphones vary but essentially, they fall under the categories of condenser or dynamic microphones. Condenser microphones provide a more accurate sound with a smoother frequency response and a higher output. They are intolerant to moisture and require a powering voltage from either the mixer (phantom power) or a battery. Dynamic microphones are simpler, cheaper and more robust. They do not require a powering voltage but the sound quality is very slightly poorer than a condenser. Other types (which are rarely used in broadcasting) include ribbon, shotgun and piezoelectric.

All microphones have directional properties, such as cardioid, omni and figure of 8, to name just three. Cardioid microphones pick up sounds in front of the microphone and attenuate sounds from the sides and rear. This way, extraneous sounds are not picked up. Omni directional microphones pickup sounds from all directions, which is generally undesirable. Such sounds are generally muddled and increase unwanted echo effects. Figure of 8 mics pickup sounds equally from the front and rear, severely attenuating sound from the sides, but this is used to good effect in drama applications.

A broadcast microphone is normally cardioid, meaning that it picks up sounds from the area in front of the microphone. There are also highly-directional microphones (hyper cardioid and shotgun); these pick up only sounds within a very narrow angle in front of the mic. Video camera microphones usually fall into this category.

In our studio, we use a variety of different types of microphone. Our most used is a £350, AT4040 made by Audio Technica. Many radio stations also use the AT4040 alongside hundreds of others. Major recording studios will invariably include the Neumann U87 in their stock because it is a standard by which all others are judged. Their £2000 price tag is, however, a limiting factor.

In order to not become consumed in a stressful "which mic" quandary, setting yourself a sensible budget and speaking to an expert helps. Allowing £100 to £350 is more than enough for a good condenser microphone, and you can pick up a used one for a lot less on eBay. We found a Behringer C1 broadcast microphone, for example, for less than £40. Other budget suggestions include: SE Electronics SE2000, AKG C3000, Rode NTK and the Shure KSM27. This does not preclude at least 50 alternatives from other manufacturers. Keep in mind that there is no "best microphone." If you talk to a radio engineer, producer or visit a microphone forum, you will soon learn how varied views can get about which mic is best for which application.

To save you time, we found The Mic Store or A to Z mics to be very helpful. They will understand what you are trying to achieve and recommend the best one for you and your budget.

Step 2: The Mixer

You will need a mixer in order to connect all your various sources and send them to your computer. Essentially, everything plugs into your mixer: headphones, microphones, sound sources such as CD and MP3 players and so on. The mixer connects to your computer via an interface or USB.

We recommend a USB mixer because it connects to your PC easily, but non-USB mixers can do the job equally well using the right cables. One budget example is the Behringer Zenith 1204 USB Mixer. This also has switchable "Phantom Power" built in, which is useful, as condenser microphones need it.

You only need a mixer if you want to play music from other sources. If you just want to connect a microphone to your computer for speech, you can purchase a microphone and a pre amp that is compatible.

A mixer can cost anywhere from £80 to any limit you set. We recommend speaking to the company Studio Spares (www.studiospares.com), as we have found them particularly helpful.

Step 3: Audio Sources

For music, we might recommend buying two CD players or a double CD player that you can plug into your mixer. Studio Spares could recommend a professional or DJ-type CD system that you could plug into your mixer. However, you only really need two audio sources, which can be anything you can lay your hands on. You could plug an MP3 player into one input of your mixer and your phone into another if you really don't feel the need to go all out, but the more "studio like" your environment, the better you will feel.

There is also software and a number of apps, which are used for the same purpose as audio sources. For example, you could download an app for your tablet then connect that to your computer to play music in. This suggestion might require a dual sound card in your computer, as you will be asking the computer to both play audio and record it at the same time.

Some voice-overs and speech presenters just use a USB mic and use only that as their home studio. For them, they need a simple, fast way of sending a microphone signal to a computer and they import music later, post recording. There are certain USB microphones, some of which are remarkably good, which record into the actual microphone itself.

Regardless of what you decide to use, probably the most important investment will be recording software.

Step 4: Recording software

The radio industry uses a number of hardware and software applications for recording and producing on-air material. The most popular two are Pro Tools by Avid and Adobe Audition. Beginners can use the Adobe product just as they can Pro Tools but the Adobe product is cheaper. Pro Tools is one of the world's most comprehensive and advanced editing platforms and also requires a small amount of hardware to run it. Another example is Audacity, which is an open source free recording and editing software application.

The world of editing software is vast and like microphones, audio sources or mixers, discussing which is best would fill an entire book. Our recommendation might be to pick one that has good access to training. Thankfully, people on YouTube have recorded many "how-to" video guides for every conceivable software package, and by simply watching a few of these, you can quickly decide which of them you prefer.

Learning how to use recording software that is most commonly used in radio stations and studios will become an invaluable skill. Spending time learning how to edit and manipulate audio on an industry standard application might sound boring, but take our word for it; this training might also be the most valuable thing you could learn in broadcasting.

Step 5: Sound treatment

When planning to record in a non-professional studio, it is sensible to consider the room acoustics. Radio studios have specially-designed doors; they have false walls and ceilings, treated floors and even special, slanted windows. Even the wood used in studios is carefully chosen, as well as the carpet and what wall treatments. Radio and recording studios are built to keep outside sound out and inside sound in.

Before you call the architect, you don't need to go to these extremes at all when thinking of creating a home studio, but thinking about some sound deadening or "room treatment" is good to keep in mind. Microphones tend to pick up room "ambience." This can create a rather unprofessional, characteristic echo in your recordings. If you are setting up in your bedroom, you likely don't want people to know that.

Surfaces affect sound, and all surfaces treat sound differently. Hard straight, surfaces repel or bounce sounds whereas soft materials or curved surfaces absorb and deflect sounds. As absorption is what you want, you can achieve a certain amount of absorption with furniture and soft furnishings, such as cushions or drapes.

If you live in an old house or a conversion apartment with high ceilings, your sound treatment is likely to be more challenging, but assuming you don't, purchasing acoustic panels can help a great deal. It can also help if your studio microphone set up is facing a corner of a room rather than a flat surface or your studio is situated in the smallest room in the house.

If you use "sound panels" as your key phrase, a quick search on eBay or on Studio Spares' website will provide lots of results and ideas. Sound paneling and room treatment is a vast area so try your microphone out first and see how it sounds; you might be lucky and have enough furniture in the room to get by.

There are also some specially made sound booths or devices that you can purchase depending on your needs. You can spend anything from £100 to £20,000 or more on room treatment but we also know "record at home" presenters who use settee seat cushions or record under a quilt for reasonable results, although this is clearly not ideal for the most comfortable performance!

Summary

Obviously, the most authentic radio-environment-mock-up scenario is to connect your headphones directly to your mixer and listen to both music and your microphone as it records into your editing software.

Your in built speakers on your computer will be ample for listening back to your recordings or practicing editing, but you can purchase some "powered" speakers and plug those into your mixer if you want something more comprehensive or would like your studio to really look the part.

Building a studio at home can be modular; you can do as little or as much as you wish. Calling some of the equipment providers will give you great insight into what you might need to get started and how you might set it all up. There are also experts on radio and broadcast forums that know how to do things like this in their sleep, and you might prefer to spend your time researching qualified people who can advise you on a bespoke option. You might even be able to find a local engineer, producer or presenter who can do the whole process for you for a small fee.

The essence of having a studio, or at least some form of home setup, is merely one avenue you can take, although we do strongly recommend acquiring and learning audio editing software. Our principal reason for recommending studio facilities is so that you can get as much practice as possible if there is nowhere else you can develop your skills. The fun you will have alongside the practice earned will be well worth the money.

The essentials of practice

Professionals have the luxury of daily practice. Even the most famous household name presenters sounded different earlier in their careers. We once heard a national breakfast show guy play old clips of himself, ridiculing how he used to sound. This is an example of how practice can make you unrecognizably better over time. Like the presenter here, not taking yourself too seriously is really important, and at the beginning, being able to laugh at yourself is a valuable faculty.

Contrary to what we are led to believe, practice not only makes perfect but it actually makes talent. Stars are rarely born. While some people are born with extrovert or introvert personality traits and some people have a natural aptitude at learning faster than others, there is no greater route to mastery than practice. Practice and the application of unquestionable determination for improvement will always amount to better results than talent alone.

Nobody is born with the talents of a world-class broadcaster, but we may be born with the capacity to desire it enough. This principal applies to everything and to every occupation. Tiger Woods is said to be the world's best golfer, yet he was not born with more golfing powers than anyone else. He himself reduces his success down to sheer hard work. In "Talent is Overrated," by Geoff Colvin, the author debunks the idea that people are born with more talent than others and promotes the belief that practice is really more important than anything else. He writes, "Great performers isolate remarkably specific aspects of what they do and focus on just those things until they are improved; then it's on to the next aspect."

Another well-known philosophy explores that being one of the world's best at anything can be a simple matter of putting in the hours. The viewpoint is based on the fact that 10,000 hours of practice at anything can make you one of the world's masters in that subject. Introduced as a concept by Malcolm Gladwell, in his book "Outliers," he presents evidence to substantiate how practice really does make perfect. As Gladwell explains, "Practice isn't the thing you do when you're good, it's the thing that makes you good." Even when you succeed and are working as a broadcaster, every day is practice and every day adds to your "flying hours."

The flying hours analogy is useful in terms of reducing your early frustrations. Knowing you will have to diligently put in the hours before you achieve results can prepare you to manage your expectations. Most of us sound terrible at first and would shiver at the thought of letting people hear our early attempts at being a presenter. If you light-heartedly accept that this might be the case and know that it will all improve with time, your early experience will be much more enjoyable and more of a challenging journey of discovery than an embarrassing ordeal.

In specific terms, one of the great advantages of endless practice and experimentation is that this helps you learn to become more real, as we explored earlier. Hearing yourself through headphones at first is very disconcerting but becomes less so the more you practice. This new radio person you are hearing in your headphones throws many presenters off and it takes a considerable number hours to direct your attention away from how you are sounding and toward what you are saying.

Hearing your voice for the first time through a professional condenser microphone and then through an EQ chain and an Optimod is surreal to say the least. An Optimod is a device used by some radio stations to "process" the signal being broadcasted. A presenter has an option when on-air to monitor what is being broadcasted to the transmitter or from the transmitter. To the transmitter, sounds quite ordinary and flat, and from the transmitter, sounds boosted and marvellous. Engineers will probably disagree with this, but they probably won't be reading this book, so it's ok.

One presenter told us how he was thrown off guard even after 10 years of radio experience. He told us of a large flagship station that had such good sound coming from the transmitter that it would put him off his links and he would stumble on his words. He was so busy marvelling at how different he sounded that he would regularly lose his concentration. He described it as almost trying to speak at the same time as hearing someone else talk in his headphones.

You, too, are most certainly going to be tempted to focus to "how" your voice sounds rather than on "what" you are saying, but the earlier you break this habit, the faster you will improve. Eventually when accustomed to your "radio sound," you'll be concentrating on what is of the utmost importance, which is what you are intending to say. Practice will help you learn to switch off your inner critic and concentrate only on your intent and your material.

The business of presenting

Radio stations employ most presenters as freelancers on a self-employed basis. In some cases, freelancers are given contracts; in others, not. Whenever someone is self-employed or a freelancer then he or she is actually a business. This is how you should treat both yourself and the process of becoming a presenter. It will help you make better decisions now and as you progress through your career. Many seasoned presenters still fail to see themselves as trading businesses, and this lack of insight leads to mistakes—sometimes catastrophic ones.

All businesses have to make money to survive and all businesses have to do marketing, accounts, set goals, business plans and so on. Your business plan is to earn money as a presenter. If you are at the start of your career, you are at the start of your business.

Like every business start-up, you might have to put considerable work in before you reap the rewards. You need to set milestones, work toward targets, stay on focus and manage your expectations, just as you would if you were planning on being a fruit seller, for instance.

If you were starting out as a fruit seller, you might first aim to sell only two pieces of fruit per day. You would not expect to have your fruit in 700 stores in the first year. It is always best to set achievable, small goals and keep your expectations reasonable.

Case Study - A frustrated presenter came to us for assistance. She was adamant that she was capable of working at her hometown's radio station and wanted answers as to why she was not getting success.

The truth was, her hometown radio station also happened to be one of the biggest stations in England, and she didn't have the necessary skills or much experience. We explained that, just as she wanted to work there, so did people more experienced than her who had more to offer.

We helped her understand the major flaw in her business plan, which was that she didn't really have one! She had set the bar too high, too early. We might as well be advocates of unlimited potential and we encourage people to dream big, but in business there are also fundamental rules in play which must be followed in order to achieve success. The TV show Dragons' Den in the UK (or in the US, "Shark Tank") springs to mind here; the greatest inventions on that show are utterly hopeless without solid business substance.

Anyway, back to the girl who came to us for advice. Instead of shattering her well-meaning ambitions, we explained that, in her case, her business plan needed new ingredients, patience, experience, flexibility and humility. We illustrated that with these components in place alongside some of the basics in this book, her chances of realising her goal had potential.

Like this example, try not to expect too much too soon. If you are starting out, forget working on the most popular station in town for now. This is way too high a goal and there are far more qualified people also wanting a job there. There is nothing more frustrating for radio management than handling applications from the overly optimistic. Save your one shot at getting their attention for when you know you are really ready.

As a business, you will be invoicing radio stations, and they will be expecting a service from you in return. As they are the ones paying you, they will have the right to determine what service is provided by you and how you provide it. If you were a curtain-maker, for example, and your client wanted red curtains, you would make red curtains. If you deliver orange curtains or think you can sway the client into buying orange, you will lose the client or they will buy curtains from someone else. This insight goes back to correctly understanding your target station and realising that, although creativity is an important, even essential, element in broadcasting, it is paramount to keep your client, the radio station, and their expectations at the forefront of your business dealings.

Like any start-up, there is also research, marketing, learning, gaining experience, listening and becoming a smart businessperson to take into account. Patience is important. This is a career and not a whimsical endeavour, so you can afford to consider playing the game long-term. Adopting this long-game approach will allow you to ensure the mistakes you make early on have less impact later. In other words, try not to alienate the boss of the biggest radio station in town by sending a demo too early on in your career if one day you want to work there. Choose to make your initial mistakes in less important roles or on less important decisions. You can achieve a lot more in life by doing things slowly and mindfully than you can by trying to make life go faster.

If you treat yourself more like a business, it will also help you disassociate from the negative and focus more on your achievements. If you like, you can treat your role as a presenter as a separate entity from yourself, and this level of objectivity will help you distance yourself from rejections and depersonalise the growth process. It will also enable a good amount of professional distance so you can analyse, learn, change and adapt.

Businesses constantly measure their results; they have tangible lists of customers and leads. They know when they are doing well and when they need to make changes. Businesses should know why they are not selling and look for ways to improve. Surviving businesses are the ones that are the most flexible in their approach to meeting goals. They look at all aspects of their operations non-emotionally and are able to devise survival and regeneration strategies accordingly. Businesses who are not able to objectively appraise every aspect eventually fail. The level of importance you place on your role, as a business manager, will directly affect your level of success.

Alternatively, as a suggestion, rather than a business, you could also see yourself as though you were a product. The launch of your career could be treated as though it were a product launch. Your job might be, then, to create a product that people want to buy—one that would change until people wanted to buy it, or one that is different enough to create a strong desire or demand. Your product would have a unique proposition or solve a particular problem. It would have one clear strategy for taking it to market and another for retaining its market position.

The business of radio

Just as targeting is important in terms of your demo and approach to radio stations, it is also important to understand the business of radio and how it works.

At the time of this book's writing, there are a number of radio groups that collectively own a number of radio stations each. Some have lots of stations: others, not so many. Groups come and go, and stations change hands or names. Not only do radio stations change hands or names but the people who work in them also change or move on.

In terms of the industry landscape, imagine the UK as a cake and several owners divide the pieces of the cake up. Doing your research into who owns what is easy and should be one of your first tasks in understanding the business of radio. Each owner is different and has different strategies, management structures and talent acquisition requirements.

Some radio stations have local management teams and others have regional management teams. Larger groups have been known to have a national programme manager; this is often referred to as the Group Programme Director. While in many cases, for significant slots, he or she will have to be involved with who gets what job, the local programme director or manager will always be your initial point of contact.

Research is part of the journey and like any job interview, when you turn up and know nothing about the company, it can look bad. Do lots of research and learn the differences between each company and how they do things. Understanding who owns what, why they do what they do and what their business model is are of complete importance.

Networking

The term networking is obviously important, and we will detail this in the promotion section. Networking in radio is another term for syndication. It means that content is broadcasted from one location to several locations (stations) at once. Most, if not all, companies have network content, and they broadcast a single show to multiple stations they own simultaneously.

You should try to be aware that if you want a slot that is currently networked you will find it harder, so it's useful to know which stations run network content and which do not. This will save you the embarrassment of trying to persuade a station to employ you for a show that does not actually exist at that location. Do note, at the same time, that because network shows appear on more than one station, more experienced presenters are most often chosen for these roles.

Networked shows require additional presentation skills. Some might require a presenter to implement "split links" and some have different "clocks" than their regular shows.

Split links allow a presenter to simultaneously broadcast different messages across multiple transmitters. They are useful if a radio station is broadcasting on numerous frequencies in different areas, but a specific message needs to be broadcast to only one area.

Clocks

Clocks, for simplicity's sake, refer to typical hours of radio programming and how content is structured. They are designed to plan, regulate and formulate radio station output. A clock determines song positions in the hour, commercial breaks, news, presenter links and, occasionally, link guidelines. A clock is given to a presenter for each hour and includes everything needed for a show. Having one makes a presenter's job very easy because everything they need for the show is all there in front of them.

Obviously, like a real clock, the sum of its segments amounts to exactly 60 minutes. Each segment on the clock is predefined, calculated and timed. There is a designated start time and duration time for each event on the clock; this might include news, travel, weather, sport, songs, commercials, presenter links and so on. Provided the presenter follows guide timings, each hour runs smoothly. A presenter has to keep a calculated check on the current time on the studio clock (the big round thing that tells the time) and his show clock. This process is also called "backtiming."

Backtiming

Backtiming is the term, which describes the time management system used by radio. It enables presenters and producers to arrive at specific junctions, such as the news or an ad-break at exact times. In a typical radio clock, pre-calculated timings are placed next to each event in an hour. These timings are often crucial to ensure that hours run efficiently to time.

There are calculators that can be purchased which allow you to do calculations in time format, and most play-out system screens do this for you. There may come a time when you are required to do it by hand, however, so it's a useful thing to learn.

Play-out systems

Theoretically, play-out systems can be any form of hardware or software that converts a signal and renders it ready for broadcast; CD players are one such example. However, in broadcasting, the term

refers specifically to software that is responsible for playing all media from the studio to the transmitter.

Play-out systems are extremely common in radio, and although there are more than one type of system, their functions all include playing audio, recording content, categorizing audio and automating programming. Hypothetically, a play-out system could be seen as the entire radio station in a box.

They can be pre-programmed to perform complicated segues (joining songs together) or to play hours and hours of content. Some radio stations programme their systems to run on automation 24 hours a day. Each system runs from a central computer, which can be accessed, by a number of its clients in the radio station. Content is loaded onto the main database, and then the radio station programs it to create playlists and clocks—this process can be done ahead of time, even weeks in advance.

Knowing various play-out systems and how to operate them on-air is important. While you don't need to learn them all, not being familiar with at least one is likely to be a significant disadvantage.

The main play-out systems you will most commonly come into contact with are as follows, in no particular order: VCD Dira, Myriad, encoDad, RCS Master

Control, RadioMan, Genesys, Audio Vault, RCS Zeta and Coolplay.

Learning even the basics of one system will give you an overview on the overall play-out software function. Some of the companies that make the

systems run direct training courses, and some of the presenter courses mentioned earlier will also teach you play-out systems. Again, look on YouTube for relevant how-to videos or visit manufacturer websites for training course information.

Show prep

As the term suggests, this is what radio refers to as show planning. Fail to prepare, prepare to fail, etc. The best breakfast shows often spend longer preparing their shows than they do broadcasting them. Prep can be the devising of content and topics, setting up callers, production elements, features or even just thinking about links.

On commercial radio stations, presenters are required to be at the radio station with enough time prior to their show in order to prep correctly. In this case, often the presenter will peruse his pre-planned show clock on paper, look for opportunities within it and/or plot locations for specific links. Breakfast shows tend to prepare the following day's show immediately after each show.

RAJAR

RAJAR stands for Radio Joint Audience Research and is the official body in charge of measuring radio audiences in the UK. There are currently approximately 310 individual stations on the survey and results are published every quarter. These results determine everything for a radio station, particularly how much money the radio station can make.

Although there are other methods for measuring listener numbers, habits and trends, Rajar is the industry standard barometer. It is important to you because many stations hire and fire presenters based on Rajar results. Visit the RAJAR website for more detailed explanations (www.rajar.co.uk).

Promoting Yourself

When you have created your demo, you will need to begin the process of marketing and promotion, just like a business. All businesses have to factor in promotional costs, and if you are serious about your career, you should think about spending between 5% and 10% of your salary on continuous promotion or development; this is also a general business rule of thumb. Once you have a stable source of income, you can however reduce this to around 2-4%.

There are times in the radio industry when many presenters are likely to all want the same job(s), so the most astute ones will devise better and more efficient ways of getting their name circulated. Of course, there is no greater promotion than referral, and this is why it is important to focus on being the best you can be in every position you find yourself in.

Promotion and marketing can be simplified best with the well-known business phrase, "cost per acquisition." Cost per acquisition means the cost of acquiring a customer, a sale, a job, a contract or even a lead. Many presenters, even professionals with years of experience, don't understand this principle, so your awareness of it already puts you in a better position.

Everything you do toward reaching any goal will always have a cost association. It might be going for a meeting with a programme director, the cost of your time and attention as you send out industry emails, making phone calls, designing websites and so on. These all contribute to calculating your "cost per acquisition." Cost per acquisition is also something to factor in your accounts, and arguably anything that is a direct cost in relation to you running the business is tax deductible so be sure to keep all your receipts and paperwork. One of the reasons that the website Radio Talent was created was to reduce the cost per acquisition costs for presenters and other talent.

While it can be easy enough for you to research who the decision makers are and start an independent marketing campaign of yourself, you should consider every possible smart marketing option or networking exercise.

A website like Radio Talent (http://www.radiotalent.co.uk) was designed to store talent "in the cloud," so that management are always able to keep track of talent from one place. It also enables programmers to make thoughtful evaluations on the talent landscape, without any of them knowing. This is one of the reasons why highly experienced people also have presence on the website.

The presenter pays for a personal page on the website in the same way someone might pay to sell a car on a site like Auto Trader (http://www.autotrader.co.uk). Included in the fee is the ability to upload to and amend his or her own Google friendly "mini website," get free advice and career guidance and be listed on a platform that has earned trust through consistency. The website works upon a passive marketing principal, which is explained in a moment.

The presenter does not have to design and pay for their own website design, coding, amendments, and search engine marketing. Rather, they simply pay for their page each year that they want to use it. Their fee also includes traffic to the website that has been cultivated over the years. While having your own website is a reasonable idea, having no visitors to it makes it less value for your money. The website does have a personalised website building service as well, but you might also know someone who can build you a great website for free.

In the early or intermediate stages of your career, you need maximum exposure of your work for as minimal an investment as possible. Even seasoned broadcasters have made costly mistakes by ignoring the power of passive marketing.

One definition of passive marketing is when something is being promoted without any or much effort from the source and/or intended benefactor of the marketing. A savings account works analogously. The longer you save, the more interest is earned, all while doing nothing. Just as a savings account earns interest, so does marketing a business. (Yes, we know nobody earns interest on his or her savings today, but you get the idea.)

Viral emails and videos are classic examples of passive marketing. One person makes a video, and everyone else spreads it for them. Having a page on a website visited by thousands of passionate radio experts is one way to secure yourself and your career passive marketing on a small scale.

Passive marketing creates a buzz. This buzz helps with fostering recommendations. Recommendations are the best types of marketing. Radio Talent essentially increases your chances because one Tweet, Facebook or Email share of your page could develop your career.

This website also has another unique quality in that it enables presenters to be discovered during a round of talent scouting by employers. Talent scouting is never advertised and a presenter cannot be included in a round of talent scouting if he or she is not in the site.

The radio industry changes quickly. One minute, each station has managers who can make decisions about hiring; the next minute, many decisions are made strategically at a higher level. Managers move around, industry roles change, people leave, and just keeping up with who is in charge and where can be a full time job. Similarly, it is just as hard for managers to monitor the skills and movements of hundreds of suitable presenters around the country. Radio Talent provides a stable platform where presenters can always be found in the same place.

Even presenters who are under contract have pages on Radio Talent. Contracted presenters still have to advertise their businesses independently. Operators never discourage a supplier (as this is what you are) from remaining in the public domain for marketing or awareness purposes. This would be rather like asking a builder working on your house to remove his Yellow Pages ad or a station asking a presenter to sack their agent whilst they are under contract.

The Radio Talent website has been responsible for creating huge salaries in both radio and television, and most of its members continue to invest in their pages every year. This is because they calculate their results on a cumulative investment basis. In other words, whatever contacts they may not reap in the first year simply adjusts the percentage or cost per acquisition for the following year.

Globally, your promotion and marketing will be a continuous effort whenever you have goals, so a proper plan is advisable. Times have changed, and while you can certainly email mp3 demos to programme managers, so can everyone else. Your chance of making an impact is reduced using this method simply because it is accessible to all.

Many use their Radio Talent page to help increase impact. On one page, a person's whole career is in front of the prospect, including their pictures, which helps with another marketing system known as "recall."

In marketing circles, recall is when a person remembers an item after being exposed to it. Marketing companies and businesses work on helping potential customers to recall their product or service. There is a famous comparison website which uses an opera singer as part of its marketing. Know the one? This is an example of recall working perfectly. Radio stations also use recall as one of their own marketing principals. Their theory is that the listener must hear content that helps them remember the radio station or elements of it.

Years ago, presenters and voice-overs sent promotional items to employers in fancy envelopes. They sent them chocolates and created strange campaigns designed to promote themselves. Largely speaking, this old-fashioned approach makes presenters look less professional and perhaps egocentric, so these techniques are not at all advised.

Some presenters use their actual shows to build marketing campaigns that boost their awareness as well as that of the radio stations. You will have heard of all manner of crazy stunts that have made presenters famous or notorious. Others make sure every show is so good that managers are always talking about them. "You're only as good as your last show" is a phrase used by many seasoned presenters who know the value of marketing. And speaking of passive marketing, nothing spreads faster than news of a person doing something outstanding.

Years ago, a presenter named Andy Hollins on the radio station Power FM, created an enormous marketing buzz by perfecting a radio feature called Love at Eleven. The feature involved callers choosing songs for their loved ones, but Andy had a unique ability of creating enormous reaction and emotion from his callers. Often they would burst into tears or open their hearts in such a compelling way that radio management all soon knew who he was. A more famous example is that of Simon Bates, whose delivery of his "Our Tune" feature made him one of the most famous presenters in the world. His magical storytelling ability had the industry talking for years. Of course, both these presenters have so many other skills, but these examples illustrate the power of passive marketing. To them, they were simply doing their show but the returns were exponential.

Always think of marketing as an essential part of your career. This will avoid being unpleasantly surprised one day to find out just how few are aware of your work. Those much more experienced than you will testify this to be something they sorrowfully encountered far too late in their careers.

Finally, when it comes to making an approach there are going to be times when you need to write letters or send emails. Although it sounds blindly obvious, never, ever send a standard email to a radio station. Always, always make it personal. You would be surprised at just how many people send a non-articulate, standard email to a radio station with their demo attached. This is highly unprofessional. Find the person's name you want to contact, refer to the station and why you want to work there, refer to something you heard on air or just be honest. Ask questions in your contact correspondence, which might encourage a response, make observations or pay genuine compliments. Below are two ideal templates, which might work better for you than a standard email. You might want to change them, however, just in case lots of people have read this book!

Example 1.

Dear Name,

As it has always been a goal of mine to work on your presentation team, I have taken the liberty to record a 90 second demo for you, which reflects my interpretation of Station Name.

I wanted to make sure that I sent an accurate representation and have taken considerable time researching this endeavour. If you could spare the time, I would therefore be very grateful if you might be willing and able to provide any thoughts or feedback as to how close I might be to your desired style and content.

I appreciate just how busy you are, and so with your consent I might drop you a line in a week or two to see if you have had the time to listen.

Learning from you would be a great opportunity, and I look forward to the possibility of hearing from you.

Yours Sincerely...

Example 2.

Dear Name,

Although we do things differently on Station Name than you do at Station Name, I am keen to get some useful pointers from you if you could spare a moment or two.

My attached presentation demo illustrates what I am doing at present, and I am enclosing this for your attention purely to gauge your reaction on my delivery, content or sound.

Your advice would help me make the necessary adjustments required, as I would very much like to be considered by you in the future as a candidate for your team.

Accordingly, I would greatly appreciate your guidance and look forward to your thoughts.

Yours Sincerely,

Your Name

Telephone number

Link to your Radio Talent page, website, or demo

Agents and getting an agent

An agent is not especially required at this stage in your career. Irrespective of popular myth, you really only need an agent when you reach a noteworthy level. Making the decision to get an agent is also a puzzling one. You can only get an agent when you are at a certain standard, but when you are at that standard you possibly don't need one. Having an agent can work both for and against you.

Let us explain. Like yourself, an agent is a business, and he or she is concerned (perhaps primarily) about his or her income. Agents make money providing a service by charging commission on the work they procure. Normally their commission ranges from 10% to 20% plus VAT. The VAT takes a significant portion if you are not VAT registered—on a £20,000 contract, the agent could get up to £4,800. Some agents, however, do have lower rates of commission.

Agents normally invoice your client (the station), then pay you minus their fees. Their fees include one or more of the following benefits:

1. A listing on their website

2. The agent's relationships with key management

3. Contract negotiation on your behalf

4. Time and attention dealing with you and your affairs

5. Possible proprietary industry information

6. Image benefits of being associated with them

There are some agents who are connected very closely with a number of high profile management, such as those at national stations. These agents are excellent choices, especially as it is almost impossible to be taken seriously by a national station without one. In many respects, therefore, even getting an agent of this calibre can be seen as an achievement all by itself. That said, landing a high calibre agent does not automatically guarantee a rite of passage.

In radio, the relationship between you and your employer is important, so cautiously consider the implications of adding a third person into the relationship. For obvious reasons, if you secure a job at a radio station yourself then it is advisable to keep that relationship separate from an agent. We once interviewed two key programme managers of large commercial networks on the subject of agents. While both of them admitted to having a positive relationship with agents and extoled their virtues, they also felt it was disrespectful when presenters whom they employed later introduced an agent. Conversely, in our interviews with national public service stations, it was clear they preferred, and were much more accustomed to, working with agents.

Do note that some agents charge a monthly fee to be registered with them. A few have even been known to request a percentage of a presenter's existing earnings in return for registration.

Agents have been responsible for changing the lives of presenters by finding them openings they would never have found themselves, but don't worry if you don't have an agent, as just as many presenters have done this alone. You should see agents for what they are: businesses, rather than entities solely invented for your future development. Just as they can help you further your business, they need to know you can further their careers. If you are lucky enough to make contact with one early in your career and get signed, be prepared for something very exciting, as they probably have plans for you!

There are good agents and bad agents, and it can take years to get signed by either. Some people have waited up to ten years to be signed by a reputable one. They are efficient and essential at certain times in a career; they are not essential or even necessary for creating one, but they are all very useful. Most of them are nice people and experts in radio, so they can give you really helpful advice. Making every agent aware of your work is definitely something you need to add to your promotional strategy.

At this point, it is worthwhile making the distinction between agents for the procurement of presenter work and agents that deal with TV or voiceover work. Most voice or TV agents are worth their weight in gold. This is because they have access to contacts who simply will not deal with you independently. Here, it's also worth challenging a common misconception; namely, that having an agent necessarily leads to voiceover work or TV. Sadly, this is not the case. Every presenter can't just move into TV or voiceovers any more than every voiceover or TV presenter can do radio. They are completely separate fields and for the early part of your career, it is best to treat them as such.

In consideration of the possibility that you will approach an agent when you feel ready, here are some useful tips:

1. Approach an agent for the right reasons: for example, if you truly believe you have something unique or quirky to offer.

2. Appreciate how busy an agent gets and how many people contact this agent with the same goal as you. Ask for opinion and guidance rather than representation.

3. Ensure you are ready to be listed on the agent's roster and that the agent understands your goals and thinks they are attainable.

4. Understand that all agents have a policy on when they take on new people, and it is rare for them to deviate from that.

5. Note that if there is someone similar to you on their books, they will be less inclined to sign you. What unique value are you bringing to their business?

6. You only need an agent when you are ready; when you are ready, persuading them to represent you will be much easier.

7. Agents need to earn money and so investing time in someone who cannot guarantee them any revenue is a risk they have to consider carefully.

8. Try not to be jealous of peers who may have agents. In the real world of radio, having an agent is not always better than not having one.

9. Some management prefer not to deal with agents and prefer to have a relationship directly with their contractor. If you have specific management as a target, learn whether or not an agent would be useful to procure this position or not.

Rejection

Regardless of how you approach a radio station, there will always be three factors that will determine your success. The first is the recipient's opinion, the second is if you fit, the third is timing.

Rejection is uncomfortable, and sadly only a few managers really understand it. Rejection is one of the reasons we suggest depersonalisation, or creating a professional distance between yourself and your work. If you are able to separate your presentations skills from who you are as a person, rejections won't be an issue and can actually be a motivation to improve your skills. If, however, you develop a mind-set that your work is who you are and your happiness is dependent on your success or acceptance, your whole career will be an ordeal.

Learning to be "independent of the good opinion of others," as Wayne Dyer says, is profoundly useful in entertainment and media. That's not to say that anyone should parade around with their nose in the air or use arrogance as protective camouflage. It simply means knowing that if you are in a room with ten people, there are likely to be ten different opinions of you. None of them are more important than yours.

As we discussed, businesses look at rejection impersonally. Not winning a sale is a form of rejection to them, but it's nothing personal. They just study the rejection and look for ways to change. This is a great way of processing any rejection you come across. It's nothing personal. In actual fact, the more virtuous among us can choose to see rejection as a gift; imagine how useful companies would find it if their customers all clearly pronounced their rejections.

If we had our way, everyone would consider their rejection parameters in consideration of people's feelings. A little careful wording and compassion takes the same time as rudeness; we have been, at times, utterly dumbfounded at how some handsomely paid managers have addressed presenters. Being a freelancer does not reward you the same rights as an employee, and sadly there are a few industry professionals who interpret this as a license to be discourteous. If you come across this, it's a lesson to stay as far away from them as possible and perceive their rude rejection as a special sort of gift in that you are liberated from the possibility of working for someone who feels entitled to be unnecessarily callous and blunt.

There will be times in your career where you will be ignored. You might contact the same person several times in a year and they might deliberately ignore you each time. This is possibly the most impertinent form of rejection and so you have to learn to develop an empowering way to process it. Ignoring the fact that someone ignored you can be a very powerful technique. If you are ignored, it helps to try and imagine that this person fully contemplated your application and was about to write you a thoughtful and helpful response, just before something serious happened and their attention was taken away. Remember, humans aren't normally deliberately unkind to each other; there is always a reason behind a person's behaviour. They could be under immense pressure, having a bad day or simply think that they are unable to articulate why you are not suitable for them. They might think the kindest way to give you feedback is to give you none and sometimes they are right.

Even though people can be unfairly rude or aloof, it is also important to recognise that how we are treated can, at times, be directly correlated to how we approach people. If you emailed a person with spelling errors or bad grammar, with a demo that was not targeted correctly or you failed to engage them, can you honestly expect them to respond? They are employed to run their own businesses rather than help you run yours. As a suggestion, however, we have found that fewer people will ignore a very articulate letter on quality paper or an exceptionally well-crafted email.

Another very inspiring way to view rejection is to treat it as a blessing or an indication that a change of approach or direction might be required. When we deal with people who are upset because they didn't get a job they applied for, we simply tell them that it's just a useful reminder that the universe has other plans for them. Learning where you are not going to work actually helps you find out where you are going to work.

It's important to focus on what can be learned from each rejection experience and how it can be used as an advantage or opportunity. An aircraft in flight is 90% off course during its journey, but it always reaches its destination. The pilot notices off-course feedback from his environment and makes small adjustments along the journey to ensure his overall success.

Sometimes making light of rejection also helps, as does putting yourself in the position of the recipient. When someone knocks on your door at home selling something you don't want, you are not always the most considerate when shutting the door in his or her face.

A great analogy is that of products. Not everyone drives the same car or lives in the same type of house or uses the same shampoo. Like products, not everyone will find you to be his or her preferred choice, but there will always be a buyer somewhere for your product, if it's good. The invention of the smartphone is a fascinating example. When the first smartphone was invented, it was inconceivable that anyone would choose any other type of phone. It also seemed like a pointless exercise for any other manufacturer to try and compete with this new device, but they did. And while a few brands of smartphones retain the major market share, customers are still buying almost all varieties, copies or expressions of the original one. Opinions are just that: opinions. Use them to your advantage.

Final thoughts

There is only one person responsible for moving forward after reading this book, and that person is you. You are the person who can actually apply this information and really absorb what it can do for you. Two people can read the same book and achieve two different results, and it really depends on the actions that they take based on the information they have learned.

Reaching your goals is both about absolute clarity of purpose and manageable, realistic expectations and timelines. It is about flexibility and changing your approach; the more flexible of any two people will be the most successful. Just as a palm tree survives a storm because of its flexibility, you too can bend and stretch to withstand adversity and achieve your goals.

When any one thing seems to not be working, look for how you can adapt and try something else. Be ready to change your approach, adjust your goal or adapt. To paraphrase Einstein, the definition of madness is someone doing the same thing over and over expecting a different result. Never lose sight of your ultimate goal but always be prepared to change it or your approach to attainment.

You are about to undergo a journey: a real path of discovering your strengths. You will meet management who will baffle you; you will be rejected, ignored or even insulted along the way. Your unwavering nature and flexibility will overcome all of this. You will take every knock in stride and understand that each bump in the road reminds you that you are still moving forward.

See your desired end result every day and visualise yourself as having already accomplished it. What does that person look like? How do they conduct themselves? Become that person in advance.

When we started in radio, industry information was hard to come by; it was a secret society, an exclusive private members club. We wanted access at all costs and gaining it was tough. Our learning curve was steep, and our desire to improve was agony. There was no one to tell us to relax, and no one to help us understand the virtues of practice and patience or that it all unfolds in the goodness of time. If this book has given you even one hint you can work with and build upon, we have succeeded.

Working toward any new goal or embarking on something you are really passionate about can lead to despair. While having an insatiable appetite for something is what creates our drive and desire, it can also be destructive. When we learn that less effort is often what creates better results, our achievements become more fun and in turn more achievable. Sometimes we even treat the attainment of a certain goal as our life defining purpose, but we fail to remember that as we go through life we change.

What we think we want today may not be what we want tomorrow; therefore, being rigidly devoted to one expression of success can be counterintuitive.

Radio is supposed to be fun. Be proactive all the time, but above all be light-hearted and enjoy the journey. Showbiz and entertainment is one of those fields where the most successful tend to have the thickest skin. While the successful are driven, they also take themselves less seriously and as a result are less completely attached to the outcomes. Just do what you love, have fun and watch it all magically unfold in-front of you. Confucius says "Choose a job you love and you will never work a day in your life."

We wish you luck and all green lights for your onward journey.

Homework

In no specific order, here are 40 useful things you might like to consider now or in the future.

1. Sign up for the radio newsletters from the website Radio Today (www.radiotoday.co.uk). This will keep you informed on the latest relevant topics in radio.

2. Join the radio forum Media UK (www.mediauk.com) so you can begin to engage in some Q+A with forum members. Keep an eye on their job section and Radio Talent (www.radiotalent.co.uk) for jobs and opportunities.

3. Create an excel sheet or elaborate word document to outline your business and career goals and put it somewhere you can see it so you can measure your progress and remind yourself to stay focused.

4. Create your own database or customer contact sheet, so you know who to contact, what they do and when you last spoke to them. Before long, you will have a large contact list of useful people. Knowing when you contacted them and what was said will ensure you don't pester them and help you remember key details that you can use in future correspondence or conversation.

5. Never send quirky gifts or promotional items to radio stations to attract attention.

6. If you're self-employed, you are responsible for paying your own tax and National Insurance contributions. You'll need to keep business records and details of your income so you can fill in an annual Self Assessment tax return. You may also

need to register for VAT if your earnings reach a certain level.

7. Never allow your goals to consume you. A goal is best set with less attachment to its outcome.

8. Always ask for feedback, advice or opinion. This sounds better than asking for a job.

9. Resist applying for jobs you are not sure you are really ready for.

10. Read "How to win friends and influence people" by Dale Carnegie. It contains the most profound, obvious and common-sense advice for dealing with people that you will ever read. The more you absorb the information in this powerful book, the more amazing your life will become.

11. Adopt an attitude of learning as much as you can. Offer to help others and they will fall over themselves to help you.

12. Search online for the audio editing software we mentioned and learn the most commonly used one. The same applies to play-out systems. The more confident you become in the operation of these things, the more confident you will feel in a studio.

13. Visit Tune In Radio (www.tunein.com) and spend time searching for your favourite stations or those that play your favourite music. Start listening actively rather than passively and see if you can start to recognise patterns. Really absorb as much as you can about the stations, visit their website, read their tweets and know as much as you can before approaching them directly.

14. Read more. Read more newspapers, articles, reviews and books. Expand your view of the world and your vocabulary. Visit the "smart-thinking" sections in the bookstores and see what interests you.

15. Find a mentor and model yourself after them. There will always be people who have travelled the path you are about to take. Some mentors might be delighted to offer you some helpful guidance or even some contacts.

16. Develop ways to turn yourself into a person who is driven by purpose rather than ego. Avoid naysayers but if you can't, find a gift in every negative comment.

17. Know there is no such thing as failure. There is only producing results. Failure is when you make a mistake and fail to learn from it.

18. Learn as much as you can about the career history of the people you want to work with or for. They will be flattered you care.

18. Never blanket email prospects with CC or BCC. Personalise every email as much as possible. If emails are not working, send an eloquent letter.

19. Listen to radio stations where the presenters work voluntarily, particularly specialist music stations. Note how genuine their passion and knowledge of music is. Note how much fun they seem to be having. See what you can learn from this.

20. Talk to your friends who are not working in radio and ask them what they like about their radio stations, their favourite breakfast shows or songs. Listen to

how they articulate and observe how they perceive radio, study how much they care and what they care most about. Compare that to your thinking about radio. Gaining an insight on what listeners want helps you quickly grasp how best to communicate.

21. See if there is a way you can take part in a local breakfast show as a regular caller.

22. Are there any other jobs around radio stations volunteering or otherwise that can help you enter the environment? Being in the environment alone provides exceptional context and helps develop industry contacts.

23. Have your demo professionally crafted and evaluated by experts such as Radio Talent, who understand the current trend for presenter skills from the industry.

24. Study the concepts of listener demographics and skews. Some radio stations are skewed towards males, others females, others youth, others mature. See if you can identify the differences between a male skew and a female skew in terms of presenter content and music choice.

25. Do some research on music scheduling software, such as GSelector4 (www.rcsworks.com). This software is one of the most widely-used music scheduling applications for radio stations. In very simple terms, it categories and defines the flow of songs on air and contributes critically to how a radio station sound is created.

26. Record amusing or interesting messages and send them to your friends, instead of emails. If you have

presenter friends or individuals who would appreciate this form of contact, this can be a very fun pastime.

27. Never, ever speak over more than 10 seconds of a song ending and if a song comes to an abrupt or definite end, always wait until it's finished. Even seasoned professionals forget to respect the music they are playing.

28. Deliberately talking up to vocals is something to be used extremely rarely. Never fill.

29. Learn which radio groups own which radio stations and who the key managers are. Media UK is a perfect resource for this.

30. Ask as many people as you can how they got their first break in radio or how their career has unfolded. Every person you speak to will provide valuable success clues, if you ask the right questions.

31. Start becoming an observer of people and their conversation topics. Keep your ear close to the ground and notice hot topics that people are talking about. Tweet trends and Facebook conversations are also good subject starters for radio.

32. Watch famous interviewers and how they work.

33. Download speech-based podcasts that discuss a subject that interests you. Absorb speech content as much as possible and as often as possible. Play these in your car; use your car as a university.

34. Regularly read stories on news websites out loud to yourself. A great deal of presenting will include reading scripts, so learning to read and not sounding like you are reading is an important skill.

35. Practice links with and without headphones and compare the differences in the end results, the ultimate goal being sounding natural.

36. Work towards having a permanent web presence with your contact details and demo.

37. Never take yourself too seriously; every journey is easier when you are having fun.

38. Ground yourself by taking an interest in other people's stories and marvel at the world's many talented people on sites like YouTube.

39. Put aside 10% of everything you earn. As a freelancer jobs will come and go and this can be very hard (another book perhaps) but saving a little for those inevitable lean times helps you stay on the path you have chosen rather than worry about your paycheque.

Printed in Great Britain
by Amazon.co.uk, Ltd.,
Marston Gate.